UNDERSTANDING
JUVENILE DIABETES

HEALTH MATTERS

BY
HOLLY DUHIG

BookLife
PUBLISHING

©2018
BookLife Publishing
King's Lynn
Norfolk PE30 4LS

A catalogue record for this
book is available from the
British Library.

ISBN: 978-1-78637-336-6

Written by:
Holly Duhig

Edited by:
Kirsty Holmes

Designed by:
Drue Rintoul

CONTENTS

Words that look like **this** are explained in the glossary on page 31.

WHAT IS DIABETES?

Diabetes is a health condition which stops the body being able to use the energy we get from our food. When we eat, our bodies take glucose from our food and **convert** it into energy. Glucose is a type of sugar and it fuels our body just as petrol fuels a car.

If you have diabetes, it means your body has trouble absorbing the glucose in your blood and using it for energy. This leads to a lot of sugar remaining in the blood, which can cause a range of health problems. It is important that people with diabetes keep a close eye on their blood sugar levels, so they can avoid these problems.

Diabetes in children is often called juvenile diabetes. There are two types of diabetes: type 1 and type 2. Most children who are **diagnosed** with diabetes have type 1 diabetes. Type 1 diabetes is often **genetic**, meaning it can be passed down through families. Type 1 diabetes is also a life-long condition, meaning it can't be cured. However, it can be treated so that people with diabetes can still live long and healthy lives. Type 2 diabetes can also be genetic but it often develops when a person gets older and can sometimes be caused, or made worse, by having an unhealthy lifestyle.

THIS MAN HAS TYPE 2 DIABETES.

FACT

ABOUT 10% OF PEOPLE WITH DIABETES HAVE TYPE 1 DIABETES.

WHAT CAUSES DIABETES?

Our bodies are made up of trillions of cells. They are the basic building blocks of all living things and they all have different jobs to do. One thing they all do, however, is take in glucose from the blood and convert it into energy. It is the job of insulin, a special **hormone** made by the pancreas, to let glucose into the body's cells. It is like a gatekeeper, or a key to a lock. Type 2 diabetes happens when the body doesn't make enough insulin, or the insulin it makes doesn't do its job properly.

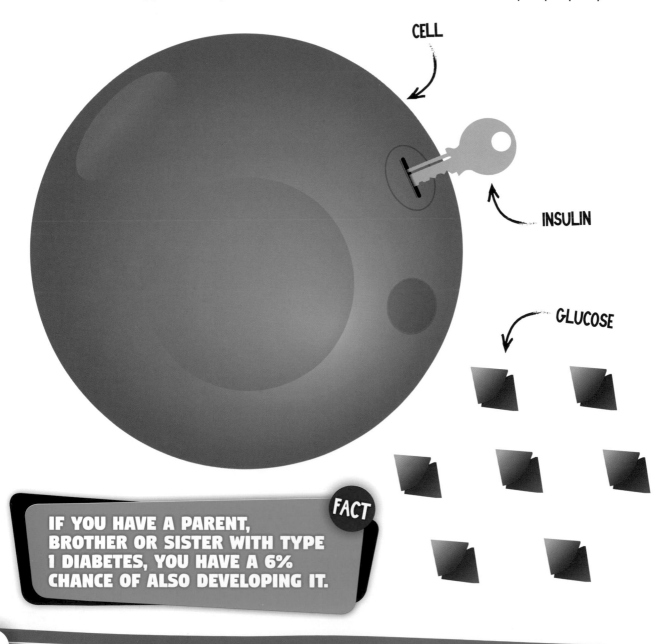

CELL

INSULIN

GLUCOSE

FACT

IF YOU HAVE A PARENT, BROTHER OR SISTER WITH TYPE 1 DIABETES, YOU HAVE A 6% CHANCE OF ALSO DEVELOPING IT.

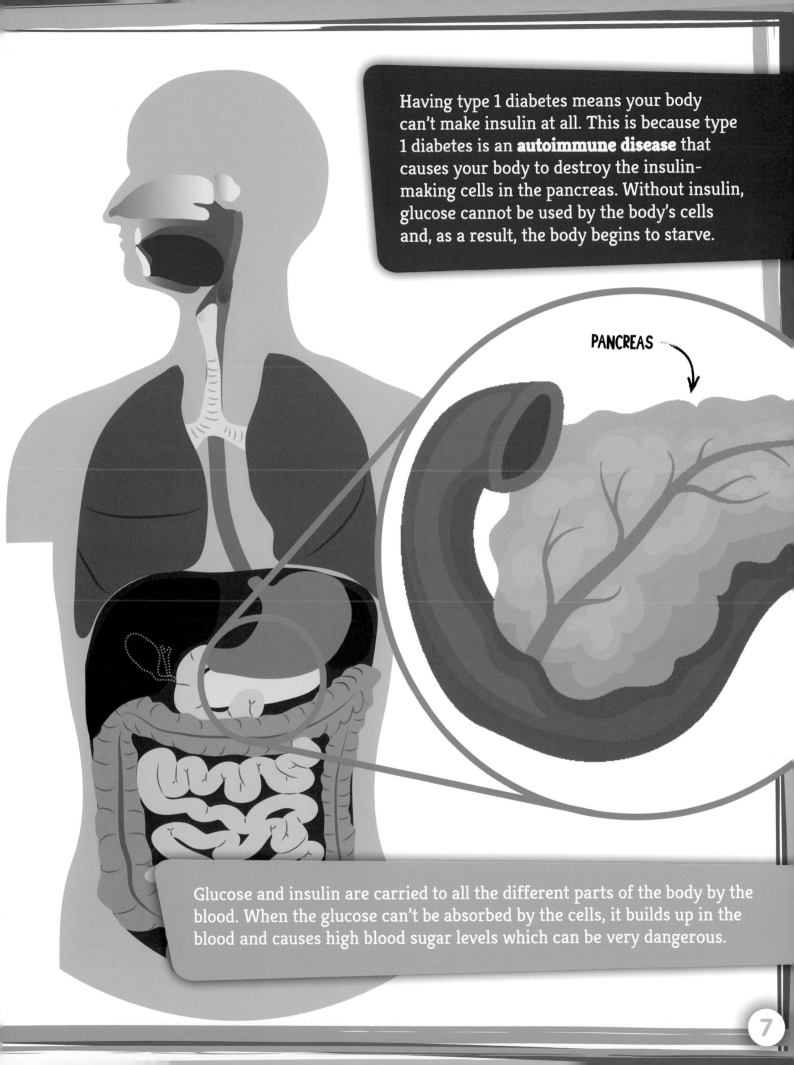

Having type 1 diabetes means your body can't make insulin at all. This is because type 1 diabetes is an **autoimmune disease** that causes your body to destroy the insulin-making cells in the pancreas. Without insulin, glucose cannot be used by the body's cells and, as a result, the body begins to starve.

PANCREAS

Glucose and insulin are carried to all the different parts of the body by the blood. When the glucose can't be absorbed by the cells, it builds up in the blood and causes high blood sugar levels which can be very dangerous.

HYPERGLYCAEMIA

The proper word for high blood sugar is hyperglycaemia (say: hi-per-gly-SEE-mia). Hyperglycaemia has many **symptoms** that are often warning signs of diabetes. One of these symptoms is needing to drink and pass urine (pee) a lot. This happens because your body needs to get rid of all the excess glucose somehow. The body is very clever and makes you feel thirsty so that you can flush out the extra sugar in your system with water. When checking for diabetes, a doctor might ask you to give a **sample** of your urine, or they might do a blood test. These are both ways of checking your glucose levels.

Another symptom of diabetes is feeling hungry all the time and needing to eat a lot. This happens because your body is not properly absorbing the glucose in the food you have already eaten so it tells you to keep eating more and more. Despite making you eat more food than usual, type 1 diabetes can actually cause you to lose weight. When your body is not getting the nutrients it needs, it will burn the fat stored in your fat cells for energy. This means you are likely to lose weight. Being underweight can be very unhealthy.

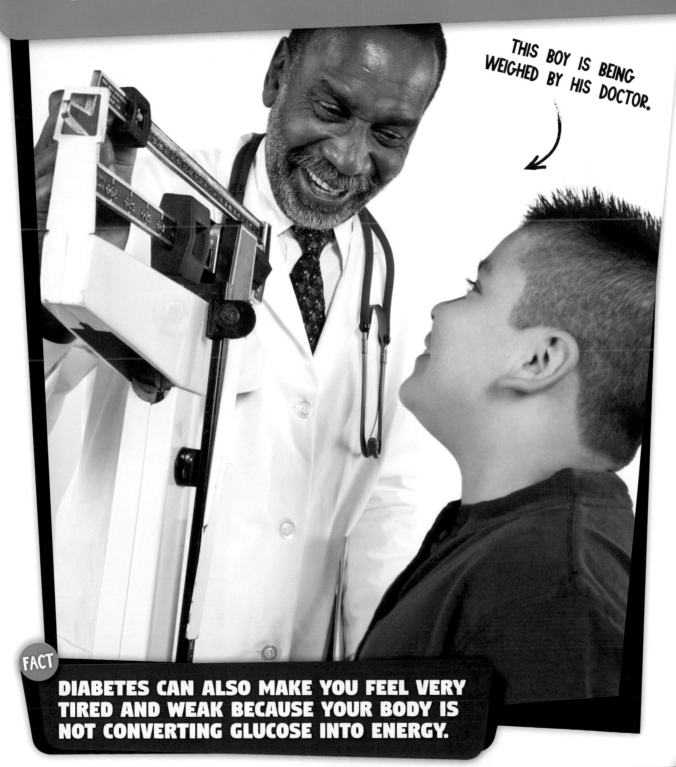

THIS BOY IS BEING WEIGHED BY HIS DOCTOR.

FACT

DIABETES CAN ALSO MAKE YOU FEEL VERY TIRED AND WEAK BECAUSE YOUR BODY IS NOT CONVERTING GLUCOSE INTO ENERGY.

How Does Hyperglycaemia Affect the Body?

Hyperglycaemia can do lots of damage to the body if it is not treated. It can damage healthy body **tissues** and organs. The body has many organs, such as the heart, lungs and brain, each of which do a different job. Most organs are made up of cells which need insulin to let the glucose in. However, some organs, such as your heart and kidneys, and some blood vessels are able to absorb glucose straight from the blood, without insulin. If there is too much glucose in the blood, these organs can absorb too much of it, and this can damage them.

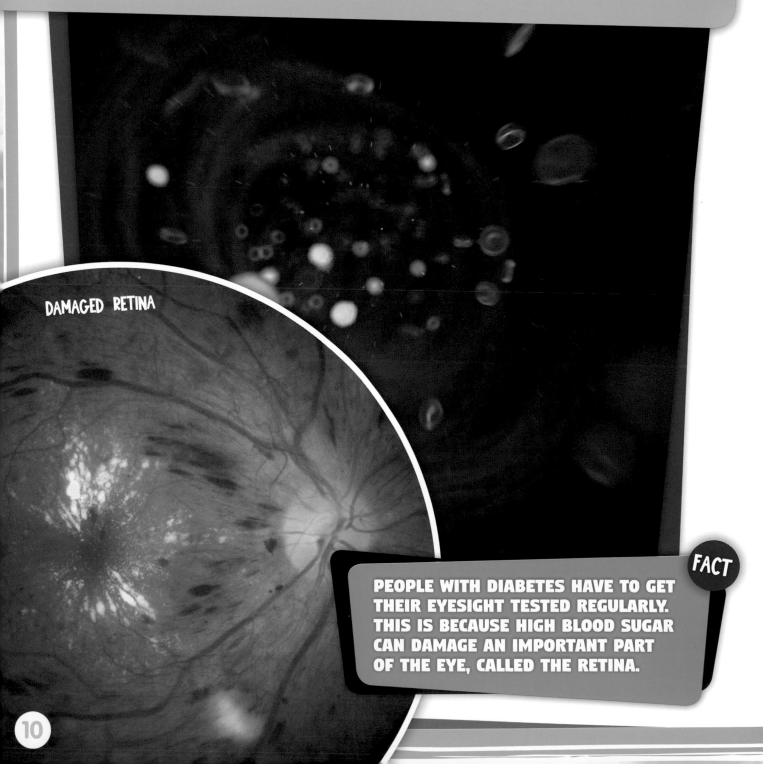

DAMAGED RETINA

FACT

PEOPLE WITH DIABETES HAVE TO GET THEIR EYESIGHT TESTED REGULARLY. THIS IS BECAUSE HIGH BLOOD SUGAR CAN DAMAGE AN IMPORTANT PART OF THE EYE, CALLED THE RETINA.

Ketoacidosis

When your blood sugar is too high and your cells are not getting enough glucose, your body will start to burn fat for energy instead. When it does this, it produces **acids** called ketones. Too many ketones in the blood can cause the blood to become too acidic and lead to ketoacidosis (say: key-toe-acid-o-sis). Symptoms of ketoacidosis include vomiting, fainting, having fruity-smelling breath and breathing very fast. It is possible to tell if someone is suffering from ketoacidosis by testing their urine for ketones.

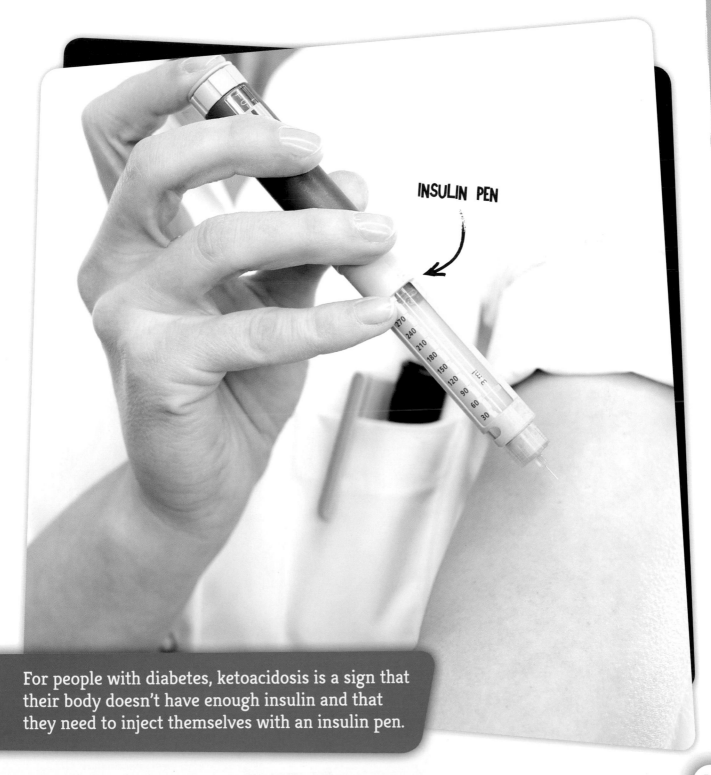

INSULIN PEN

For people with diabetes, ketoacidosis is a sign that their body doesn't have enough insulin and that they need to inject themselves with an insulin pen.

HOW IS DIABETES TREATED?

Blood Sugar Tests

Diabetes is monitored with blood sugar tests and treated with insulin injections. People with diabetes have to check their blood sugar levels regularly. They do this by pricking their thumb or finger with a **lancet** or lancing device to produce a tiny bead of blood. This blood is then dropped onto a testing strip which is attached to a monitor. The monitor will tell them what their blood sugar level is. Having to prick your finger every day can take a little bit of getting used to when you first get diagnosed. But don't worry; lancing devices are designed to cause as little pain as possible.

THIS BOY IS USING A LANCING DEVICE.

TIPS FOR TESTING

1. **ALWAYS REMEMBER TO WASH YOUR HANDS BEFORE DOING A BLOOD SUGAR TEST. THIS STOPS GERMS ON YOUR HANDS FROM GETTING INTO YOUR BLOOD WHEN YOU TAKE THE TEST.**

2. **NEVER REUSE A LANCET. ALWAYS GET A CLEAN ONE OUT.**

3. **USE DIFFERENT FINGERS EACH TIME TO STOP ONE FINGER GETTING TOO SORE.**

4. **TO MAKE TESTS AS PAINLESS AS POSSIBLE, ALWAYS PRICK THE SIDE OF YOUR FINGER RATHER THAN YOUR FINGERTIP AS THERE ARE FEWER NERVE ENDINGS THERE.**

CONTINUAL GLUCOSE MONITORS

Instead of using lancing devices, some people choose to use a continual glucose monitor (CGM) to measure their blood sugar levels. Continual glucose monitors use sensors which are placed just under your skin. Instead of measuring how much glucose there is in your blood, they measure how much glucose there is in your interstitial (say: in-ter-STI-shull) fluid. Interstitial fluid surrounds the cells in the body. The sensors are attached to a device which can be clipped onto clothes or kept in your pocket. The device displays your blood sugar level.

BLOOD GLUCOSE MONITORS ARE SMALL ENOUGH TO FIT IN YOUR POCKET, AND CAN BE ATTACHED TO THE SENSOR WITH A TRANSMITTER, WHICH SENDS THE INFORMATION FROM THE SENSOR TO THE MONITOR.

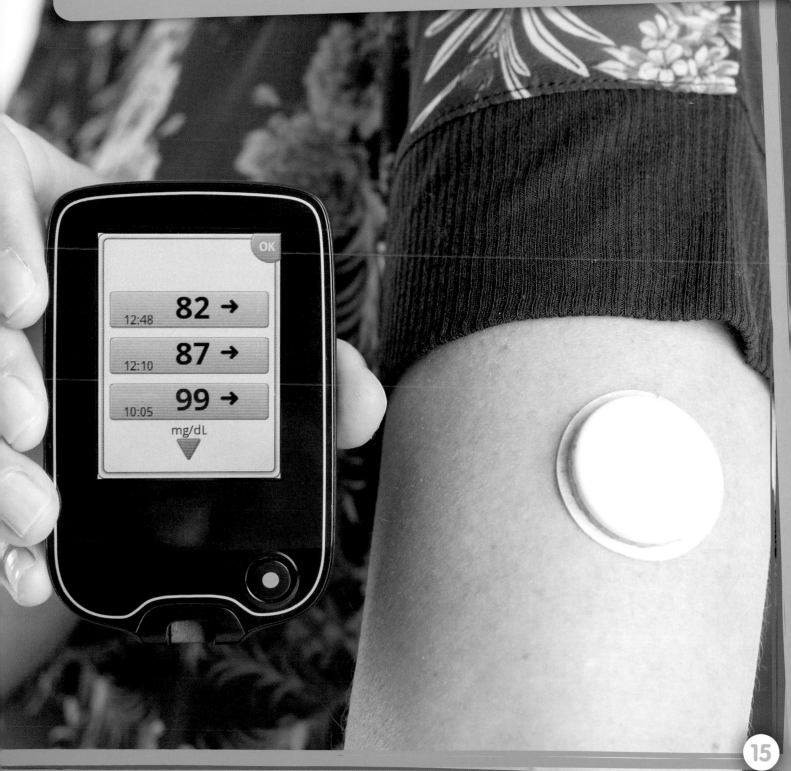

The sensors only need changing around once every seven days. CGMs help people with diabetes to monitor their blood sugar levels while they're sleeping. They can even be set to beep when blood sugar levels are too high or low. Wearing a CGM means people with diabetes don't need to do as many finger pricks.

However, because they measure interstitial fluid rather than blood, there can be a delay of around 15 minutes in detecting changes in blood sugar levels. This means people tend to prefer taking a blood test if they need quick results, for example after exercise.

OK

12:48 **82** →

12:10 **87** →

10:05 **99** →

mg/dL
▼

INSULIN INJECTIONS

As well as taking regular blood tests, people with diabetes also need to inject themselves with insulin. This is because having diabetes means that you have to do the job that your pancreas would normally do.

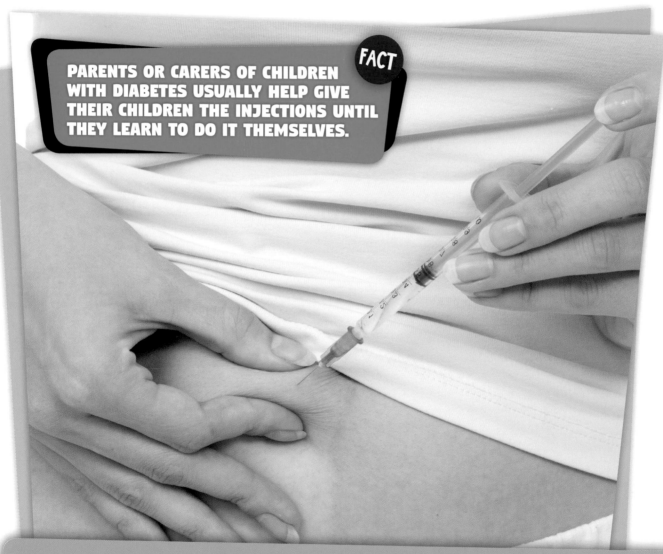

FACT

PARENTS OR CARERS OF CHILDREN WITH DIABETES USUALLY HELP GIVE THEIR CHILDREN THE INJECTIONS UNTIL THEY LEARN TO DO IT THEMSELVES.

Before performing an insulin injection, you must first make sure the area you are injecting is clean. Most people inject into a fatty part of their body such as their stomach, thigh or buttocks. If people inject into the same part of their body over and over again, fatty lumps might appear. These are not harmful, but they can make it harder for your body to use the insulin. So, if lumps appear, it is important to inject into a different area.

Insulin can be injected using a syringe, but it is usually injected using an insulin pen. Insulin pens have very small needles. These needles are covered with a cap because they need to be kept clean, but also because needles can spread **infections**. If someone was to accidently get pricked by another person's insulin pen, they could get an infection from any germs and **pathogens** that are on the needle. Insulin pens also have a dose adjustment dial at the top so you can make sure that you are injecting the right amount of insulin. Before injecting, it is very important do an 'air shot'. This is where you shoot at least two **units** of insulin into the air to make sure there are no pockets of air in the needle.

DOSE ADJUSTMENT DIAL

CAP

NEEDLE

AIR SHOTS ARE IMPORTANT BECAUSE IT IS VERY DANGEROUS TO INJECT AIR STRAIGHT INTO THE BODY.

CASE STUDY: MILES

My name is Miles and I have type 1 diabetes. I found out I had diabetes when Mum took me to the doctors' surgery. She took me because I was feeling sleepy all the time and once I even fainted at school. The doctor told me I had type 1 diabetes and that it was a serious illness but it can be easily treated. She showed me how to test my blood sugar and how to use an insulin pen. At first, I was really frightened about having to use a needle and cried a lot, but when the doctor showed me the insulin pen I realised the needle was actually very small.

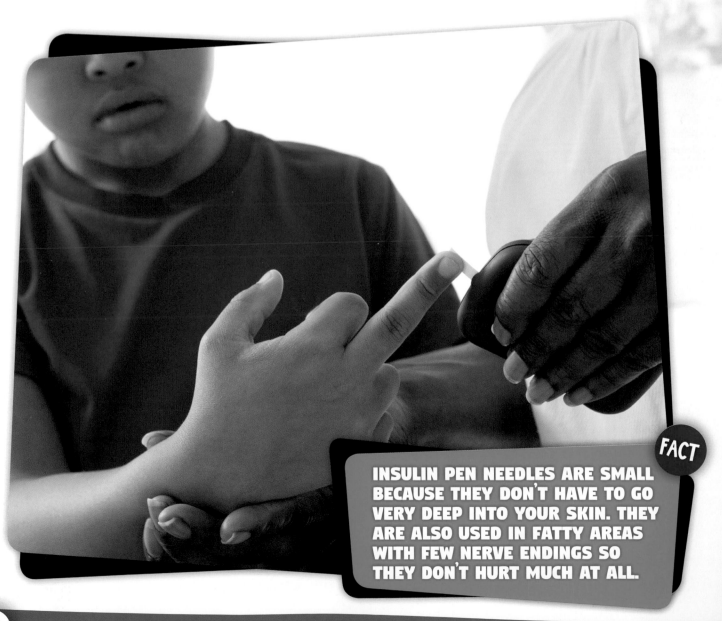

FACT

INSULIN PEN NEEDLES ARE SMALL BECAUSE THEY DON'T HAVE TO GO VERY DEEP INTO YOUR SKIN. THEY ARE ALSO USED IN FATTY AREAS WITH FEW NERVE ENDINGS SO THEY DON'T HURT MUCH AT ALL.

Because of my diabetes, I now have to be more careful about what I eat and this sometimes feels unfair. When my friends have birthdays, I usually have to test my blood sugar levels to see if I can have some birthday cake straight away or if I have to take some home with me to eat later.

Sometimes I can't eat the same amount of sweet things as my friends. I can still eat them, I just have to be careful about when I eat them. I sometimes carry fruit, chocolate or glucose tablets which help raise my blood sugar levels quickly if they are too low.

HYPOGLYCAEMIA

The proper word for low blood sugar is hypoglycaemia (say: hi-poh-gly-SEE-mia). If you've ever felt a bit shaky or weak after not eating for a long time, you have probably experienced low blood sugar. For most people this isn't a problem but for people with diabetes it can be more serious. Hypoglycaemia can give you a headache and can cause you to feel shaky and dizzy. Diabetic people might say they are feeling 'hypo' when this happens. Hypoglycaemia can be caused by injecting more insulin than your body needs, or by not eating enough food. This is why people with diabetes often carry a sugary snack or glucose tablets.

FACT

MANY PEOPLE WITH DIABETES WILL FEEL HYPOGLYCAEMIC IN THE MORNING BECAUSE THEY HAVE NOT EATEN FOR A LONG TIME.

Diabetes affects your body but it can also affect your mood. Both high and low blood sugars can affect your emotions, but low blood sugars tend to affect them more. Just like the rest of your body, your brain needs glucose to function properly. Low glucose can cause you to feel anxious, nervous or annoyed. It is very common to feel like you can't control your anger when you are hypoglycaemic and you might find yourself getting easily annoyed. It can be hard to tell when you are feeling angry because something has happened to upset you and when it is caused by hypoglycaemia. If you are diabetic and feel tired, weak or dizzy alongside these emotions, it is probably a result of hypoglycaemia.

CASE STUDY: JULIA

My name is Julia and I love to play tennis. I have become really good at it and I even play in competitions now. I have type 1 diabetes but that doesn't stop me winning! I take a blood test before matches so I know whether I need to eat something before I play. Usually I will eat some chocolate and drink some water to keep **hydrated**. Having diabetes makes me want to show people that I'm stronger than they might think!

FACT

EXERCISE IMPROVES THE BODY'S SENSITIVITY TO INSULIN SO THAT, OVER TIME, THE BODY MIGHT NEED LESS INSULIN.

IF YOU EVER FEEL FAINT, TRY TO FIND SOMEWHERE YOU CAN LIE DOWN. IF THIS IS NOT POSSIBLE, SIT DOWN SOMEWHERE COMFORTABLE WITH YOUR HEAD BETWEEN YOUR LEGS. THIS WILL GET THE BLOOD FLOWING TO YOUR BRAIN.

Sometimes, having diabetes makes me feel dizzy and tired. One day I was climbing the stairs at school when I started to feel hypo. I felt like I might faint and I knew that would be very dangerous so I sat down and asked a teacher for help. I don't like it when my diabetes makes me feel weaker than other people. However, I know this feeling only lasts for a short time and, as long as my blood sugar is normal, I'm just as strong as everyone else!

EXERCISE AND DIET

Hypoglycaemia can be caused by injecting more insulin than your body needs, or by not eating enough food. When you are diabetic you have to be careful not to skip meals or do exercise without eating afterwards because you need to replace the energy that you have burned while exercising. People with diabetes often need to eat something high in sugar after exercise. Fruits like apples and pears are a healthy way of quickly boosting your blood sugar levels.

Having diabetes doesn't mean you can't lead an active life or take part in sports. In fact, there are many famous diabetic sports stars including Olympic rower Sir Steve Redgrave.

People often think having diabetes means you always have to be on a strict diet, but this is not true. People with diabetes still need to eat plenty of food from a variety of different **food groups**. They simply have to be a little more careful than others to make sure they are balancing what they eat with their exercise and insulin levels. Whether or not you have diabetes, a healthy diet with lots of variety is important for everyone.

We get a lot of our glucose from carbohydrates, which is a food group that includes foods such as pasta and rice. Because of this, many people with diabetes like to keep track of how many of these foods they are eating and plan meals that are low in carbohydrates. Creating meal plans can be really helpful for controlling diabetes. Children with diabetes often have regular check-ups with a doctor. Doctors can help you create meal plans that are low in sugar but still include the foods you enjoy eating.

BREAD, POTATOES
AND NOODLES ARE
ALL CARBOHYDRATES.

Some people with diabetes keep their blood sugar levels stable by eating a certain amount of carbohydrates for each meal. This makes the doses of insulin they need to take more **consistent**.

Some people keep track of their blood sugar levels and inject themselves with insulin multiple times throughout the day. This allows them to be flexible with what they choose to eat and when. Other people may only inject themselves twice a day at regular times. Because of this, they might also try to eat at regular times too. People with diabetes often have to pay close attention to the labels on the food they are eating. This is so they can balance their insulin levels against the amount of sugars and carbohydrates they take in.

Nutrition Information

Typical values Per 100g: **Energy 1073 kJ** 253 kcal; **Protein 0.5g; Carbohydrate** 62.4g of which **sugars 53.6g** of which starch trace; **Fat 0.1g** of which **saturat** trace; **Fibre 1.1g; Salt trace** of which sodium trace.

Typical values Per 15g serving: **Energy** 161 kJ 38 kcal; **Protein 0.1g;** Carbohydrate 9.4g, of which **sugar** 8.0g of which starch trace; **Fat trac** which **saturates** trace; Fibre 0.3g

PARENTS AND TEACHERS OF CHILDREN WITH DIABETES WILL USUALLY HELP TO ADD UP THE SUGAR AND CARBOHYDRATES ON FOOD LABELS.

A CURE FOR DIABETES?

Luckily, the treatments for diabetes are getting better and better and people with type 1 diabetes are now able to live as long and as healthy a life as anyone else. Scientists are always trying to find easier methods of treating the condition. For example, they hope to find a way of getting insulin into the blood without having to inject it. Not having to use needles would make life much easier for people with diabetes.

As well as finding new ways to treat diabetes, scientists are also searching for a way to cure it once and for all. They hope to do this using stem cells. Stem cells are human cells that don't have any particular job and can be turned into other types of cells that do have a job. Scientists hope they can use stem cells to make the insulin-producing pancreas cells that are missing in people with type 1 diabetes. This would allow their bodies to regulate their blood sugar levels and remove the need for injections.

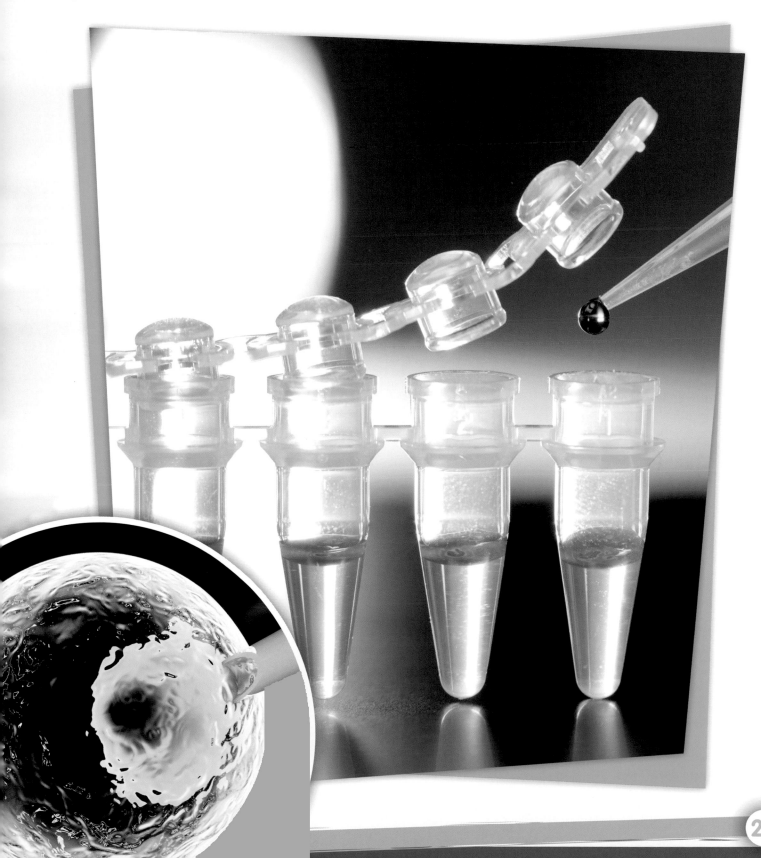

LIVING WITH DIABETES

Diabetes can be a difficult and, at times, frustrating condition to live with, but it is manageable and treatable. Many children with diabetes feel different to their friends and worry that they won't be able to join in with all the things their friends do. However, most children with diabetes live normal, active lives, even if sometimes they have to be more careful about certain things. As long as it is managed with insulin treatment, a good diet and plenty of exercise, there's no reason why childhood diabetes should hold you back.

CHILDREN WITH DIABETES WILL KNOW A LOT MORE ABOUT THE HUMAN BODY AND HOW IT WORKS THAN CHILDREN WITHOUT IT.

GLOSSARY

acids	substances in the body that are responsible for breaking down things such as nutrients and fat
autoimmune disease	a disease caused by the body's own immune system attacking its host
consistent	the same each time
convert	to change something from one form to another
diagnosed	when an illness or problem is identified by a doctor
food groups	the categories into which different foods are placed
genetic	passed down to offspring through genes
hormone	a chemical in your body that tells cells what to do
hydrated	to have enough water
infections	illnesses caused by dirt, germs and bacteria getting into the body
lancet	double-edged blade or needle used for taking blood samples
nerve endings	points under the skin which sense things like temperature, touch and pain
pathogens	organisms that can cause disease in living things
sample	a small amount of something that is analysed scientifically
symptoms	things that happen in the body suggesting that there is a disease or disorder
tissues	groups of cells that are similar to each other and do the same job
units	a single measurement

INDEX

Image Credits
*All images are courtesy of Shutterstock.com, unless otherwise specified.
With thanks to Getty Images, Thinkstock Photo and iStockphoto.*
Front Cover – Robert Przybysz. 2 – ratmaner. 4&5 – Eviart, Syda
Productions. 6&7 – Designua, Tefi, Panda Vector. 8&9 – Robert
Kneschke,. 10&11 – Sebastian Kaulitzki, Santibhavank P, Robert Przybysz.
12&13 – R Kristoffersen, Evgeniia Trushkova. 14&15 – Tyler Olson, Click
and Photo. 16&17 – Dmitry Lobanov, EsHanPhot, Rob Byron. 18&19
– JPC-PROD. 20&21 – VaLiza, DiversityStudio. 22&23 – Patrick Foto.
24&25 – Gregory Johnston, By Ollie Harding (https://www.flickr.com/
photos/paddling/6166079545/) [CC BY 2.0 (http://creativecommons.
org/licenses/by/2.0)], via Wikimedia Commons, ifong. 26&27 – Claudio
Divizia, Evgenia Sh. 28&29 – wavebreakmedia, science photo, Spectral-
Design. 30 – Robert Kneschke.